Chasing Kindness Against the Wind

By Sibel Terhaar

About the Author

Sibel Terhaar is a kindness activist and international author. Her inspirational messages on social media have motivated and captured millions of hearts looking for kindness in a challenging world.

Sibel was born the youngest of two children in Ankara, Turkey. Her parents were brought up in Eastern Turkey and were married at the young age of fourteen. Sibel had many hardships as a child. Her father suffered from many addictions and was abusive, and as a result, they lived in poverty and often went without food for days. Sibel questioned how the world could be such a cruel place; because of this, the slightest act of kindness was life-changing and felt like finding a drop of water in a barren desert.

During her teen years, Sibel was not allowed to participate in activities outside school except visiting her local library. She spent hours reading Shakespeare, King David, and many others. Every page she read was an adventure and an escape from her experiences at home, but one book changed Sibel's life: How to Win Friends & Influence People by Dale Carnegie.

Dale spoke about smiling, showing a genuine interest in people, and God's love. It was then that Sibel decided to incorporate these principles into her life. She made it her mission to engage with everyone she could and positively influence others. In college, Sibel had an opportunity to share her perspective with others as a host of a popular radio station. It was one of the best experiences in her life, and it was then that she felt she had finally found her voice.

Sibel immigrated to the United States in 2003 and started a new life with her husband as they raised a family. In 2020, during the COVID-19 pandemic, Sibel had another opportunity to share messages of hope and kindness, this time on LinkedIn. She started posting quotes about kindness and life on LinkedIn, and the response was overwhelming. Her messages resonated with many, and she continued networking and building a community of like-minded people striving for a kinder world.

Today, Sibel continues to post messages of hope and kindness on LinkedIn and other social media platforms.

"Kindness is a giant warrior
that has never lost a battle."

"The heart does not feel
complete satisfaction
without hard work.

The world advances,
develops, and aims for a
brighter future through
hard-working people."

"Creativity begins with a brilliant mind that is influenced by the ideas of other minds, unites them with harmony, and then transforms them into reality."

"When success knocks at your door, it may come as an unfamiliar face and look different than what you expected.

It is neither a friend nor enemy but instead, a traveler that has no loyalty and cares not to linger."

"We should not forget that we are all human and fall from time to time.

It is easy to fall and hard to get back up, but that is where resilience is forged, and growth occurs."

"We are in control of how we perceive our experiences and how we respond in life.

So many of us respond emotionally, without considering perspectives, and unfortunately, miss out on true growth."

"Those who dare to believe in dreams are the ones who catch the world's beauty.

They understand life, and turn their dreams into reality, despite any obstacles in their lives."

"When science and technology are not a priority, humanity's challenges are an uphill battle, and the results often lead to the grave."

"Hard work wins the race, but kindness brings the crowd to their feet."

"Always elevate your dreams and pay no attention to selfishness.

Let hope, faith, and truth be your guide. Let your life light the way for others."

"Dark days will pass with patience, mindfulness, and a shared responsibility in facing the battle as one."

"We help each other out
and lift each other up,
especially on days when we
all are hurting from the
same grief."

"A true friend walks the walk beside you, never rushing or avoiding but always supporting."

"When we walk through the darkness alone, with fearful hearts, we lose the battle.

United, hand in hand, we can overcome hardship through our shared pride in what we have in common."

"A company is like a person's character.

It will prosper if the company is honest, fair, and hard-working."

"Share your smile and let it sail across oceans, and the winds of promises will deliver it to people in need."

"If we keep our spirits up,
any battle can be won."

"You may think knowing oneself would be easy, but knowing what we're capable of and then acting on that knowledge is one of life's greatest challenges."

"Despite our cowardly enemy, who fights without motive, we can stand tall with purpose.

Through sacrifice, we can unite with a shared resilience against fear and overcome all that stands in our way."

"We must aim to achieve happiness at the intersections of love, forgiveness, and truth."

"We don't live life in fear.
We live life in the pursuit
of happiness.

We will endure, and we
will fight against COVID.

We will win the war with
our courageous army of
healthcare heroes."

"Don't be a person who is not interested in poor, orphaned, and fallen people.

Be a person who lifts people regardless of their societal status.

Love, kindness, and goodness are the best qualities of humanity."

"Forgiveness is difficult to do, but it is one of the greatest virtues.

It frees you from a heavy heart and helps lead you to a more positive and happy life."

"A broken heart can heal
with time, but clarity and
possibly regret come first.

Don't let the window of
tomorrow fog over because
a new day will come, and
the sun will rise again."

"Capability is not born from skill or experience; it is merely a choice to say yes, I can do that."

"Never give in, never stop, never bend, and never give up."

"Kindness is a pleasant partner in all things.

Lifting others with hope or sharing sorrow in a time of grief has no agenda besides comforting those in need."

"Sometimes it's best just to wait and listen.

The world is not going anywhere."

"Occupy yourself with continuous learning and positive thinking that leads to a perfect punch.

All are important in knocking out negativity in your mind."

"You can't beat working with a company emphasizing a positive work environment."

"Each day you give
someone the gift of
kindness, you light the
same gift within yourself
and shine a little brighter
for the world."

"Only a gentle heart can spout kindness and ease the pain."

"Even on overcast days, our hearts are clear and bright, shining throughout the land."

"Whether it is luck or coincidence, the mystery of why we have met is unknown, yet meaningful."

"It is our nature to bond and comfort each other when faced with hardship and tragedy.

Imagine what the world could be if we united through our aspirations and not our collective sorrow."

"We can't fully enjoy life without giving up our ego and pride.

Selfishness is the root of unhappiness.

We must hop on the right train and travel in the right direction."

"Don't underestimate the power of a good person.

If you hurt them, they may leave without hesitation and you will have suffered the loss of a good friend.

"True wisdom is gained from the clarity that comes from being broken."

"The heart can be gullible
and may seek affirmation
first.

Step back from yourself
and question everything.
Let your words rest and
find logic before speaking."

"When the world is shattered, kindness is the only path to a brighter future."

"Don't give up trying to change the direction of the world.

The world needs a straight path, and you have it."

"Help the poor in spirit when they are broken.

Nothing compares to the satisfaction from lifting others in times of need."

"Don't let the vision of a perfect outcome get in the way of completing your goals and moving on to your next great achievement."

"I will not allow fear to imprison my spirit or diminish the light within me."

"Like a lamp in the night, a true friend lights the way and brings comfort to a lonely journey.

Through joy or sorrow, the path is traveled together, and in all things, with love."

"True change is rarely accomplished alone, but the support from a loved one can move mountains and change lives."

"When your heart is burdened and filled with pain when a dark spirit follows you all day long, when depression threatens to take your soul, reach out for the hand of a loving friend.

Reach from the depths of your heart and strive to connect with a kind soul."

"Let us embody courtesy as
a noble duty.

Although the roads are
treacherous, let's continue
to show kindness and keep
our hearts positive."

"Never let misery get in the
way of joy."

"Reading the world through your own eyes will help write the next chapter in your story."

"A good man who fills his heart with kindness will bring peace to the people around him."

"Living life for others is not
a pity but a selfless virtue."

"Bruises through life's struggles begin to heal when you move forward with a positive mindset."

"All that we do, see, and hear; influences us.

Despite this, we do have control and can discern what is true and right and ignore flattering lies that persuade us into believing without first listening."

"Share your burdens with loved ones, as you would with the joy in your world.

Carrying too much of anything alone, even joy will drive the love out of your life."

"The person who lays down
their sword and gives up on
the war within themselves
will see the promise of a
new day and the world that
can be."

"Abandon the negativity
that whispers with deceit.
Leave the darkness that
welcomes despair and
embrace yourself by
believing you are more than
enough."

"Don't be the person who judges people without knowing them, only because of unpleasant emotions.

Be a person who loves people unconditionally. Because love is the greatest gift humanity has, and no one has the power to destroy love."

"Time does not care what
we have scheduled, nor
waits for our convenience.

However, cherished
memories can be a
sanctuary where time is not
invited."

"Those who don't believe in themselves will never start the race."

"The most beautiful days
are spent without regret and
worry."

"Although we can't stop time, we can breathe in a moment and spend eternity in a thought."

"Being positive never grows old and helps with being happy, meeting our goals, and getting ahead in life."

"Don't give up on all of
your hard work when
success is so close."

"A smile is a decision to set your destiny.

Sharing your smile with others is a commitment to change the world."

"The greatest defeat in life
is letting hatred take over
your soul."

"I go wherever I see a spark
of kindness.

I seek unending love.

I will gladly stay when I
find it, never to return."

"Love is a magical story
that is written by the heart."

"Love speaks louder than anything, touches the heart deeper than the harshest of words, and resurrects hope in the darkest nights."

"You can change the world.
It only takes the simple
decision to dare to do it."

"Be the one who lifts a broken world and pours kindness onto people's hearts."

"The first step towards
being brave often involves
taking a step back."

"Those who are hurting inside, do not worry, for the stars will shine, the fallen will rise, and beautiful days will be seen again."

"When your point of view collides with others, try to see all sides of the story."

"Let your soul shine with the light of a million stars and share your love as the sun shines on us all."

"I would rather run through the hottest of flames chasing after my dreams than seek the shade and dream of my potential."

"Leave the pettiness behind and follow wherever eternal grace leads you."

"True kindness is selfless and flows like a river, delivering hope to those in despair."

"The road to success is a long journey, and those who want to see results without hard work may not be willing to walk it."

"Nor mockers, evildoers, fools, thieves, players, haters, or liars can wrong us.

So long as we live with honor, kindness, and love, we shall rise, and they will fall."

"A world with no heart is of
no value to anyone."

"When people tell you it is okay to give up on your dreams, it's usually because they either don't believe in your potential or have none themselves."

"Never give up on a
promise that you've made
with yourself."

"Don't be the dreamer that only envisions the outcome but forgets the struggle it takes to get there."

"A righteous soul will
never bow to hate but is
quick to surrender to love."

"Start every sunrise with a smile and let the sunset leave you content for the night."

"There is no happiness
without inner peace."

"The only way to thrive in life is to create your narrative and be the winner in your story."

"Love cannot speak without courage, and its words are sincere yet not easily given."

"I want to spread kindness throughout the hearts of the world and smiles upon the faces I meet until my last day.

Upon that day, when my journey is complete, I only hope to look back and know I've reached my destination with my loved ones waiting for me."

"Despite everything falling around you, don't let your hope diminish within the shadows of despair.

Stand tall and be a beacon of confidence for those who walk and seek hope."

"I cannot live, watch, and
stare.

I must run after the moon,
aim for the stars and pass
by the hottest sun before
returning home with hope
in hand. "

"Let your kindness be like a flower, open and waiting for the sun to shine on a new day."

"To be a great soul, unite in love, and hold the world together."

"Life is infinitely beautiful;
always touching, consoling,
and connecting each of us
throughout space and time."

"The moment you rebel against fear, you will meet the bravest and boldest person within you."

"Hate does not have enough power to defeat love, but love has enough power to conquer the world."

"I want to seek out distant lands with meadows of happiness, valleys of hope, and a river of truth that I can sail home on and share the many treasures of love I've found."

"Silence is the hidden voice
of a brokenhearted man.

He doesn't speak his
struggles, and his heart
remains unheard."

"Forgiveness is about destroying the anger within and returning to love."

"Faith is healing your heart with God when you are defeated."

"The world is not a paradise, nor an Inferno.

Yet free will remains, and our ability to achieve greatness is more than our shortcomings."

"Reality begins the moment
you wake up."

"To me, happiness is putting the biggest smile on somebody's face and knowing that God is pleased with me."

"I don't hear the voices of
the city.

I hear the voice of God."

"As always, smile with warmness, act with tenderness, and speak with kindness."

"A great leader, strong as Iron, still bends to the counsel of his team.

Determined, and set on a clear path, but always looking ahead and adapting to their needs."

"Although I sometimes imagine a different life, nevertheless, my heart draws me back to the dream of what I can do with today."

"Goodness exists within the depths of all hearts, but the light of kindness may be lost forever when pride is king."

"Some of the most beautiful smiles are buried under broken hearts."

"Turning away from the crown may hurt at the moment but will make you stronger when your reason is true."

"My arrows are real and laced with truth, straight from my soul, and aimed at your heart."

"Many people battle with themselves, seeking their perfect self.

Few have laid down their swords and found a purpose greater than themselves."

"Let your love move at the speed of light and with endless momentum."

"Maybe it's the fire in your
heart that will burn all the
hate from the world."

"Walk with me towards a
new and kind world.

The path is long, but the
destination is forever."

"Even the hardest of hearts
can be moved by a kind
word."

"Even when you walk alone in the dark of night, the brightest star will have its say and speak to your heart and show you the way."

"The size of your audience does not determine the value of your message.

Live each day as though your entire purpose in life is to share a few KIND words with one LOST soul."

"Comparing yourself to others is a battle you are destined to lose and only leads to suffering."

"A friend is a companion through the best days and the darkest nights.

Like a lamp in the night, a friend lights the way and brings comfort on a lonely journey."

"The difference between
feeling at home or alone is
the company you keep."

"My soul has confirmed it with my heart; my purpose is to spread the message of love."

"Holding on to painful
memories only sacrifices
your future happiness."

“Try again and move boldly
towards your dreams,
leaving all your fears
behind.”

"Everyone shall find the truth in this life, and although some will run and others will walk, no one will escape it."

"Always wear the crown of kindness and walk bravely amid the unknown."

"Dwell on positive things, and you'll bring light into your world."

"Promise yourself, even when the foolish pulls you down, you will stay kind."

"The wisest mind takes the boldest action."

"Standing before your enemies shows your power, but when you forgive them, that shows your inner strength."

"Roar with all of your might against the voices of doubt. Let your confidence shine upon the providence that is set before you."

"Never waste a night with anxious thoughts on your mind but let yourself dream of a tomorrow without worry."

"I want to spread kindness throughout the hearts of the world and smiles upon the faces I meet until my last day.

Upon that day, when my journey is complete, I only hope to look back and know I've reached my destination with my loved ones waiting for me."

"Find your voice and share
it with the world!"